S 7/07 C O H O

D1220110

ZORA NEALE HURSTON

"I Have Been in Sorrow's Kitchen"

Laura Baskes Litwin

Series Consultant:
Dr. Russell L. Adams, Chairman
Department of
Afro-American Studies,
Howard University

 Enslow Publishers, Inc.
40 Industrial Road
Box 398
Berkeley Heights, NJ 07922
USA
http://www.enslow.com

"I HAVE BEEN IN SORROW'S KITCHEN AND
LICKED OUT ALL THE POTS. THEN I HAVE STOOD
ON THE PEAKY MOUNTAIN WRAPPED IN RAINBOWS,
WITH A HARP AND A SWORD IN MY HANDS."

—*Zora Neale Hurston*

Library of Congress Cataloging-in-Publication Data

Litwin, Laura Baskes.
    Zora Neale Hurston : "I have been in sorrow's kitchen" / by Laura Baskes Litwin.
        p. cm. — (African-American biography library)
    Includes bibliographical references and index.
    ISBN 13: 978-0-7660-2536-3
    ISBN 10:   0-7660-2536-5
    1. Hurston, Zora Neale—Juvenile literature. 2. Novelists, American—20th century—
Biography—Juvenile literature. 3. Folklorists—United States—Biography—Juvenile
literature. 4. African American novelists—Biography—Juvenile literature. 5. African
American women—Biography—Juvenile literature. I. Title. II. Series.
    PS3515.U789Z765 2005
    813'.52—dc22

                                                                  2005034881

Printed in the United States of America

10 9 8 7 6 5 4 3 2 1

To Our Readers:
We have done our best to make sure all Internet addresses in this book were active and appro-
priate when we went to press. However, the author and the publisher have no control over and
assume no liability for the material available on those Internet sites or on other Web sites they
may link to. Any comments or suggestions can be sent by e-mail to comments@enslow.com or
to the address on the back cover.

Every effort has been made to locate all copyright holders of material used in this book. If any
errors or omissions have occurred, corrections will be made in future editions of this book.

Illustration Credits: The Associated Press, AP, p. 102; Beineke Rare Book and Manuscript
Library Collection, Yale University, pp. 37, 52, 61, 81, 84 (left and right); Department of Special
Collections, George A. Smathers Libraries, University of Florida, pp. 21, 26, 108, 109; Library
of Congress, pp. 3, 4, 5 (left and center); 9 (left and center), 12, 14, 17, 19 (left and center), 24,
29 (left and center), 31, 41, 43 (left and center), 44, 55 (left and center), 66 (left and center), 70,
74, 79 (left and center), 86, 89, 94 (left and center), 105 (left and center); Moorland Spingarn
Research Center, Howard University, pp. 5 (right), 9 (right), 19 (right), 29 (right), 35, 43 (right),
55 (right), 66 (right), 79 (right), 91, 94 (right), 105 (right); New York Public Library, p. 84 (cen-
ter); Photographs and Prints Division, Schomburg Center for Research in Black Culture, The
New York Public Library, Astor, Lenox, and Tilden Foundations, p. 39; Photo by Carl Van
Vechten, used with permission of the Van Vechten Trust, print from Beineke Rare Book and
Manuscript Library Collection, p. 67; Photo from the Langston Hughes Collection at the Yale
Becineke Library published by permission of Harold Ober Associates, Inc., p. 48; Print courtesy
Stetson Kennedy Collection, University of Florida Library, p. 76.

Cover Illustrations: Library of Congress

Contents

Zora Neale Hurston

Chapter 1

Narrow Escape

In a remote wooded area in central Florida, Zora Neale Hurston was working undercover. She was living in a seedy boardinghouse on the grounds of a lumber camp. In difficult and often dangerous conditions, the workers at this camp were making turpentine, a product used to thin paint.

For two months in 1938, Hurston had been posing as a bootlegger on the run from the law.[1] A bootlegger is someone who makes or sells liquor illegally. Bootleggers got their name because they hid flasks of homemade liquor, or "moonshine," as they called it, against their legs in the top part of their boots.

Hurston created the disguise of the bootlegger to account for the sporty Chevrolet coupe she drove and expensive dresses she had with her. To the people at the turpentine camp, it made sense that a bootlegger would have these fancy things. But how Hurston came to have them, and how she came to be at the camp in the first place, was another story altogether.

Zora Neale Hurston was not rich. A wealthy woman in New York City named Charlotte Mason had bought everything for her. This same woman had then hired Hurston to take a road trip through the rural back roads of the South. Mason was interested in African-American folk traditions. Hurston's job was to uncover and record the traditions of the African Americans in the South.[2]

The turpentine camp workers were a mixed lot. Some were straight-arrow preachers, but others were petty crooks and a few were even prison escapees. It was the presence of these outlaws that convinced Hurston to create her cover. She knew she would be much likelier to gain their trust—and their stories—if they believed she was one of them.

In fact, Zora Neale Hurston was a writer. She was interested in gathering folklore not only because someone was paying her, but also because the vivid way of life she heard described made its way into her novels, short stories, essays, and plays.

The turpentine camp was an awful place. The workday began at dawn, and a pistol-toting boss made sure it never ended until dark. But often after sunset, and always on Saturday nights, the workers let loose at the "jook joint." The jook was the camp's informal nightclub; a plain pine cabin transformed by rowdy music, square dancing, and gambling.

On one particular Saturday night, Zora Hurston was celebrating the end of the workweek with a woman from the camp whom everyone called Big Sweet. Big Sweet was large in size and personality, and most people were afraid of her. It was whispered that Big Sweet had killed two men.[3]

Hurston had made friends with Big Sweet, taking her for drives and giving her a gift of a bracelet. In return, Big Sweet had made certain Hurston got all the stories she wanted, encouraging the storytellers even when they were not in the mood to recite.

What happened in the jook joint that Saturday night came about very fast and in the wee hours of the morning. Hurston and Big Sweet were making conversation with a man named Slim. He was one of Hurston's favorite sources for folktales and jokes.

Slim had once dated a woman named Lucy. Even though they were no longer a couple, Lucy was unhappy about the time Slim was spending with Hurston. She was so upset, in fact, that she pulled a knife on Hurston that night. Before Hurston had time to react, Big Sweet had opened her own switchblade and wrestled Lucy to the ground. The jook went wild.

In the midst of the riotous confusion that followed, Hurston narrowly escaped with her life. She had a bag packed and was behind the wheel of her car in minutes. "When the sun came up," she recalled later, "I was a hundred miles up the road, headed for New Orleans."[4]

Hurston never learned exactly how the fight ended in Florida, but she would put herself in perilous circumstances many more times in the pursuit of her art. She was daring and ambitious, choosing to defy convention and experience a full life at a time when few women took those kinds of risks.

Hurston's self-confidence had its roots in her childhood and in the rich and unusual community in which she was raised. From a very young age, Zora Neale Hurston heard the voices that would give shape to almost all the stories she would write.

Chapter 2

Eatonville's Girl

Zora Neale Hurston was born on January 7, 1891, in Notasulga, Alabama, the fifth in a family of eight children. Before her first birthday, the Hurstons moved to the place Zora would always call home, a town in central Florida named Eatonville.

Eatonville, Florida, was a most unusual place. This was due not only to its natural beauty, though it had that in abundance. Gardenia bushes perfumed the air with sweet fragrance. Oranges, tangerines, and grapefruit grew everywhere for the picking. Largemouth bass, bluegill, and alligators swam in the town's five lakes.

But the uniqueness that was Eatonville came from a charter drawn up in 1887, just four years before Zora was born. This agreement provided that Eatonville would become the first self-governed, all–African-American town in the United States.

In the years following the Civil War, the Deep South remained an inhospitable place for its African-American residents. While slavery had been officially abolished, whites still owned the land and blacks still farmed it for them. Segregation laws, known as Jim Crow laws, kept the races rigidly separate, and deadly racial violence against African Americans occurred daily.

In Eatonville, things were different. Here, the men and women who set the rules were the same color as those who were obliged to follow them. Here, unlike almost any other place in America at the time, a rich black community thrived, free from the control of white authority.

The Hurstons lived on five acres in the center of town, close to church and school. Zora's father, John, built the family's house with a sleeping loft upstairs and a wide front porch to welcome visitors. The Hurston home was a lively one, as Zora described it, "noisy from the time school turned out until bedtime."[1]

John Hurston had grown up in extreme poverty. His parents were sharecroppers, moving from one plantation to the next in search of a better living. Sharecroppers were farmers who worked other people's land and often only made enough to survive. Hurston taught himself to read and set his sights on becoming a minister. One Sunday at church, he met fourteen-year-old Lucy Potts and slipped a love note into her hymnbook. The two were soon engaged.

Lucy Potts came from a very different background from her future husband. Her father owned land, and the Potts family believed themselves to be the social superiors of the sharecropping Hurstons. Lucy's mother refused to attend her daughter's wedding.

But John and Lucy Hurston began their life together happily, and four children—three sons and a daughter— were born in the nine years before Zora came along. Three more boys were born after Zora. Lucy Hurston encouraged her children to pay close attention to their studies and above all else, to embrace life to its fullest. Zora recalled years later that "Mama exhorted her children at every opportunity to 'jump at de sun.' We might not land on the sun, but at least we would get off the ground."[2]

As a little girl, Zora liked to sit atop the fencepost in front of her house and attempt to make conversation with strangers passing by, some of whom were white. "I did not do this with the permission of my parents, nor with their foreknowledge," she admitted. "When they found out about it later, I usually got a whipping."[3] Zora's parents worried that she would get herself in trouble flaunting the dividing line society drew between the races.

Within the friendly confines of Eatonville, however, the Hurstons had few worries. Zora and the other children were looked after by a community that fiercely protected its own. Like citizens in most close-knit towns, the men and women of Eatonville shared concerns and gossip

When Zora was a child, her mother told her to "Jump at the sun!"
As an adult, left, she still liked to play and have fun.

almost every day. They met on the front porch of Joe Clark's general store.

Joe Clark was one of the town's original settlers and its second mayor. His store was, as Zora put it, "the heart and spring of the town."[4] She recalled later that "the store porch was the most interesting place that I could think of. I was not allowed to sit around there, naturally. But, I could and did drag my feet going in and out whenever I was sent there."[5]

On Joe Clark's porch, men relaxed playing cards or checkers and women did the same collecting recipes or herbal remedies. The adults offered homespun advice to boys and girls who, like Zora, lingered a bit on their way home. Zora's teenage brother received counsel on how he might grow a moustache in order to look older than his years.[6]

But it was the folktales she heard told on the general store porch that would have the most lasting effect on Zora. "God, Devil, Brer Rabbit, Brer Fox, Sis Cat, Brer Bear, Lion, Tiger, Buzzard, and all the wood folk walked and talked like natural men," she wrote later.[7] These folktales

Brer Rabbit Stories

Brer (a shortened version of Brother) Rabbit is the fictional hero of a series of stories first brought to this country by West African slaves. Brer is the slave who refuses to give in to his dire circumstances. Relying on cleverness and a sense of humor, time and again Brer Rabbit gets the better of his white slaveowner. An uncle of President Theodore Roosevelt first published these folktales in *Harper's* magazine. But it was a journalist named Joel Chandler Harris, under the pen name Uncle Remus, who brought the stories to wide popular acclaim.

Zora loved to listen to the adults in Eatonville, as they gathered on the porch of a general store like this one, sharing gossip, advice, and stories.

illustrated for Zora both the depth of her people's culture and the immense value of storytelling itself.

When she was about seven years old, Zora began to experience premonitions, or visions of future events. At night, in great detail, she dreamed of things that were yet to happen. Many of these dreams were scary, unhappy nightmares. For years she told no one of her visions because they made her feel "too different . . . weighed down with a power I did not want."[8]

One nightmare convinced Zora that she would be orphaned: "The comforting circle of my family would be broken, and I would have to wander cold and friendless until I had served my time."[9] It was not long after this vision that Lucy Hurston became very sick.

Her mother's illness was difficult for thirteen-year-old Zora. For one thing, Zora and her father had long endured an up-and-down relationship. John Hurston had never made a secret of the fact that he favored his other daughter, Zora's older sister, Sarah. Sarah was meeker and prettier than Zora and their father fawned over her, buying her dresses, toys, and music lessons.

John Hurston had succeeded in becoming a minister. He headed one of the churches in Eatonville, but his work took him to churches in other parishes as well. While away from home, he was often unfaithful to his wife. The children heard their parents' frequent arguments about this, and Zora was protective of her mother.

Of course, like most children, Zora loved her father despite her anger with him. She admired his great physical strength and his intense, charismatic personality: "He had a poetry about him that I loved."[10] Still, Zora knew, "I was Mama's child."[11]

Lucy Hurston was Zora's most faithful advocate. When her father reprimanded her, Zora knew she could count on her mother to take her side, saying "Zora is my young 'un. . . . You leave her alone."[12] More important,

Lucy nurtured the sparks she saw in Zora's independent nature. At a time when girls were not generally encouraged to think for themselves, Lucy's support was vital to Zora.

Lucy Hurston was only thirty-eight when illness overcame her. She had been sick since returning home from nursing her dying sister a few months earlier. Lucy knew she was dying now as well and called Zora to her bedside.

At this time in the South, certain rituals were followed when a loved one died. The mirrors in the house were covered because superstition held that anyone reflected in the glass would die next. Clocks were hidden because an uncovered clock was believed to permanently stop ticking at the moment of death. A dying person's pillow was removed from the bed, supposedly to ease the way into the afterlife.

Lucy Hurston did not believe in these folk rituals and did not want them observed at her death. She asked Zora to make certain her last wishes were honored. Yet when Lucy died, the mourners around her naturally adhered to tradition, ignoring the protests of a young daughter.

Losing her mother at thirteen was hard enough. To believe, as Zora did, that she disappointed her mother at the end was even harder. She wrote later, "That moment was the end of a phase in my life. I was old before my time with grief of loss, of failure, of remorse of failure."[13]

After his wife died, John Hurston quickly made the decision to send his older children away to boarding school

Zora was unprepared for the strict segregation and racism in Jacksonville, Florida. This picture shows a street in the African-American section of town.

in Jacksonville, Florida. Zora packed a single suitcase in which she stashed all her belongings and took an overnight train with her siblings.

Jacksonville was not like Eatonville: "Jacksonville made me know that I was a little colored girl," Zora would recall.[14] In all–African-American Eatonville, there had been no segregated bathrooms or streetcars. In Jacksonville, Zora was confronted for the first time in her life with the ugliness of Jim Crow laws.

Grieving for her mother and struggling to be on her own, Zora was very unhappy. Then she received news that made matters even worse. Only five months after her mother's funeral, her father had remarried. John Hurston's new wife, Mattie, was just twenty years old.

Mattie Hurston asserted herself right away. Zora's sister Sarah had left school due to homesickness. Seeing the favored Sarah as a rival for her husband's affections, Mattie insisted Hurston whip her. It was the first and last time John Hurston would hit his daughter. Sarah left home at once to marry a man she barely knew.

Zora felt the sting of her father's new marriage when he suddenly stopped paying her boarding-school tuition. So that she might stay to finish the semester, Zora took a cleaning job at the school. But when classes ended and she had no money for the train to Eatonville, Zora was faced with the embarrassment of borrowing the fare from the school principal.

Home was even more unpleasant. Zora and her stepmother fought constantly. What was likely even more difficult for Zora to accept was the change in her father. She noticed that, "He didn't rear back and strut like he used to."[15]

Zora felt unwanted and unloved. Without the money for school, she had to make other plans. Though she was not yet fifteen years old, she knew somehow she would have to make her way in the world.

Chapter 3

Second Chance

The next years were tough ones for Zora. She wanted to be in school, but her father had made it clear that he was done paying for the private academy she had been attending in Jacksonville. Free public schools existed, but for African-American students in the South these segregated schools were poorly funded, often ramshackle places.

Zora's mother had taught Zora how to read before she even entered kindergarten. As a teen, she remained an avid reader. What she missed most about being in school was having books available to her. She had no money to buy them otherwise. "I was without books to read most of the time, except where I could get hold of them by mere chance," Zora related. "That left no room for selection. I was miserable."[1]

Understandably, Zora was especially miserable because she had been forced to leave home. The circumstances surrounding this were grim; her father had chosen to make his new wife happy by evicting his young daughter. On top of this, Zora was still dealing with the aching grief of losing her mother.

She would later describe this time in her life as "haunted. I was shifted from house to house of relatives and friends and found comfort nowhere."[2] Her older brothers took her in, each for a time, but their situations were unsettled as well, and Zora was unable to stay anywhere for very long.

She needed a place to live and she needed money, so sixteen-year-old Zora hired herself out as a housekeeper. Most of these jobs did not last more than a month or so. By her own admission, Zora was "just not interested in dusting and dishwashing." Instead, she would peruse the homeowner's bookshelves, "get tangled up with their reading matter, and lose my job."[3]

For nearly eight years, Zora worked as a maid and nanny. She was bored, and more than anything else, she was lonely: "I wanted family love and peace and a resting place," she wrote.[4] At one point during this period, she felt desperate enough to move back home, despite her father's refusal to welcome her. This trial arrangement ended in bottle-throwing and a fistfight between Zora and her stepmother.

Zora Hurston chose then not only to move out, but also to leave town. She got a job with a traveling musical theater company. She was responsible for the wardrobe

For most of her teen years, Zora Hurston was on
her own, moving from house to house and job to job.
This picture was taken around 1916.

and makeup of the lead actress. There were about thirty actors in the troupe, all white, and all but one from the North.

From the start, Hurston loved everything about the job. The money—ten dollars a week—was far more than she had ever earned. The actors were interesting, friendly people. They appreciated Hurston's southern dialect and way of expressing herself. "If I got mad and spoke my piece," she said, "they liked it even better."[5]

Hurston became intimately acquainted with the backstage workings of a theater, and she learned new plays and music. As an added bonus, company members lent her books. For the first time since her mother's death, Hurston felt like she had found a home.

She stayed with the troupe for a year and a half and might have stayed longer if her employer had not decided to leave the theater company herself. The group was performing a musical in Baltimore, Maryland. Hurston's sister Sarah and her husband had recently moved there, so Hurston took her last pay and made plans to stay for a while.

At this time, the laws of the state of Maryland provided free schooling for African Americans until they turned twenty.[6] Hurston had always looked much younger than she was. Now, so that she could go to school for free, she decided to say she was only sixteen years old.

For Hurston to want to subtract ten years from her life is not hard to understand. The past decade had been enormously difficult. She had yearned to be in school since the day she had been forced to leave it. Given the opportunity to finish high school, pretending to be younger must not have seemed too large a stretch for her.

Of course, it was also much easier to tell her classmates that she was sixteen rather than twenty-six. And the story took hold. For the rest of her life, Zora Hurston would claim to be ten years younger than her actual age.

In September 1917, Hurston began night classes at Morgan Academy, the high-school division of Morgan College in Baltimore. Most of her classmates were the children of doctors and teachers. While money was not much of an issue for them, Hurston described herself as having "only one dress, a change of underwear and one pair of tan oxfords."[7] Yet from the beginning, she made friends and earned the notice of her teachers. The dean of the school helped her find a job on campus, and in two years Hurston earned a high school diploma.

In the summer following graduation, Hurston's father was killed in a car accident in Memphis, Tennessee. Zora did not attend his funeral. Perhaps past difficulties with John Hurston clouded her reaction to his death. In any event, she was focused on immediate plans for college.

Zora Hurston had intended to continue at Morgan College. A chance encounter with someone affiliated with

Howard University changed her mind. Founded two years after the Civil War, Howard was the largest and most prestigious African-American university in the country. When Hurston was told she was "Howard material," she decided to apply and was admitted for the fall semester.[8]

Howard University was in Washington, D.C., so Hurston made the short move from Baltimore. As always, she needed a job to pay for school, and she took one as a manicurist in a barbershop near the White House. Her

Hurston was thrilled to be accepted as a student at Howard University.

clients were congressmen and journalists who gave her an insider's view of goings-on in the nation's capital.

For someone who had never even imagined going to college at all, finding herself at Howard was a dream. Hurston worked diligently at her studies and was asked to join the elite literary club on campus. Formed by a young philosophy professor and Harvard University graduate named Alain Locke, this group produced a magazine called *The Stylus*.

In the May 1921 issue of *The Stylus*, Hurston published her first poem, "O Night," and her first short story, "John Redding Goes to Sea." The character John in her story is based on her father, John Hurston.

There was another man in Zora Hurston's life at this time. His name was Herbert Sheen, and he was her first serious boyfriend. Hurston wrote, "He could stomp a

From "John Redding Goes To Sea"

"Sometimes in his dreams he was a prince, riding away in a gorgeous carriage. Often he was a knight bestride a fiery charger prancing down the white shellroad that led to distant lands. At other times he was a steamboat Captain piloting his craft down the St. John river to where the sky seemed to touch the water. No matter what he dreamed or whom he fancied himself to be, he always ended by riding away to the horizon, for in his childish ignorance he thought this to be farthest land."[9]

Hurston, center, with some classmates at Howard University.

piano out of this world, sing a fair baritone, and dance beautifully."[10] Like Hurston, Sheen was the child of a preacher and working his way through school.

The couple spent much of their free time together until Sheen got a job as a butler in New York City and transferred to Columbia University. Hurston continued at Howard, though her grades outside of her writing classes were not good. By the start of the winter term of 1924, she had decided to leave Howard to try her luck in New York City, too. Herbert Sheen was part of the reason. Her new-found writing success was a bigger part.

Hurston had just received word that a story she had written, "Drenched in Light," was to be published in the December issue of a magazine called *Opportunity: A Journal of Negro Life*. *Opportunity* was one of the most important African-American publications of the day. This was a great honor for Hurston and her first big break.

"Drenched in Light" is the story of a little girl in Eatonville, Florida, who likes to sit atop the gate in front of her house and talk to the people walking past. The girl is poor, but she is happy; hers is a childhood joyfully "drenched in light."

Clearly autobiographical, "Drenched in Light" was Hurston's first published account of her hometown and the interesting people who lived there. There would be many more accounts to come, but this was the first, and this was the one Hurston would use to cannonball herself into the middle of the chief African-American literary circle in New York City.

Hurston arrived in New York at the start of January 1925, with only $1.50 in her change purse.[11] She went immediately to the offices of the National Urban League, the publishers of *Opportunity*. There she met with Charles S. Johnson, the magazine's founder and editor.

A sociologist by training, Johnson believed *Opportunity*'s mission was to advocate black equality and economic uplift and to prove black artists were on a par with whites.[12] Hurston's short story had convinced him of her talents.

Johnson told Hurston that *Opportunity: A Journal of Negro Life* was sponsoring a writing contest, offering cash prizes for the best submissions. The awards dinner would be held in a few months' time. Charles Johnson helped Hurston find a place to live and urged her to get right to work.

Chapter 4

Opportunity Knocks

F rom his offices in midtown Manhattan, Charles Johnson pointed Hurston five miles north. He assured her that she would find an apartment in a section of the city called Harlem. In 1925, the year Hurston arrived in New York City, Harlem was a lively place.

At this time, more than one hundred thousand African Americans called Harlem home. Many had recently moved from the South, seeking work and a life free from the threat of lynch mobs—the lawless groups that murdered African Americans. On a map, Harlem's borders made a mere four square miles, but this densely populated area was unique in the United States. The 1920s, when Harlem was the height of fashion, is a period historians call the Harlem Renaissance.

In Harlem, African Americans owned businesses, drove taxicabs, and joined the police force. They served as doctors, lawyers, entertainers, and ministers. There were African Americans doing these jobs in other parts of the country, but in nowhere near the sheer numbers as they were in Harlem.

Harlem's blackness was to many an oasis from an unfriendly white world. "I'd rather be a lamppost in Harlem than Governor of Georgia" was a common expression among residents.[1] In many ways Harlem, New York, was a lot like Eatonville, Florida.

On Harlem[2]

"I was in love with Harlem long before I got here."
—Langston Hughes, African-American author

"In some places the autumn of 1924 may have been an unremarkable season. In Harlem, it was like a foretaste of paradise."
—Arna Bontemps, African-American author

"Harlem, I grant you, isn't typical—but it is significant, it is prophetic."
—Alain Locke, American educator

"Harlem is still in the process of making."
—James Weldon Johnson, African-American author

"Why, it is just like the Arabian Nights."
—Duke Ellington, American jazz bandleader, composer, and pianist

Harlem was bustling with excitement during the Harlem Renaissance.

Though Zora Hurston had arrived in town almost penniless, she was far from alone. Many of the area's people found it difficult to pay the rent every month. Something called a "rent party" had become a Harlem tradition.

Rent parties were open to anyone who could pay the entry fee, which was usually an amount between a dime and fifty cents. The person holding the party collected the money, hoping to earn enough to pay the rent. Parties were typically held on Saturday nights because rents were due on Sundays. The unlucky renter unable to come up with the money often found his or her furniture on the street the following day.[3]

The parties began after midnight and continued all night, often with live music and always with dancing. Despite the prohibition laws that forbade drinking, there was plenty of liquor available, much of it made in local bathtubs.[4] The party food was inexpensive, home-cooked Southern specialties like black-eyed peas, collard greens, and sweet potato pie.[5]

Hurston was a favorite at these "flop-wallies," as they were sometimes called. She danced with abandon and told elaborate, clever stories about her childhood. One guest related years later that, "When Zora was there, she *was* the party."[6] Although Herbert Sheen had left New York for medical school in Chicago, the rent parties gave Hurston a steady social life.

Prohibition

In January 1920, the Eighteenth Amendment to the U.S. Constitution banned the manufacture, sale, and transport of liquor. But this law, known as Prohibition, was difficult to enforce and openly mocked by many. The federal government hired too few agents to police the country and before long, organized crime ran the lucrative business of making and selling illegal alcohol. Clubs called "speakeasies" served liquor to anyone who "spoke easy" enough to convince the club bouncer that he or she was not a federal agent. Doctors wrote prescriptions for whiskey, making false claims that the drink was purely medicinal. Many people made their own liquor at home in the bathtub. The Twenty-first Amendment repealed the prohibition law in 1933.

For those who had money, Harlem provided other out-standing entertainment. In the 1920s, many of New York's night owls were wealthy whites who lived far south of Harlem's 125th Street border. To these people, Harlem's people of color were exotic and its nightclubs were places to let loose. Further, Prohibition laws were not enforced in Harlem, making it a safe haven for all who wished to drink alcohol.

During her first months in New York, Hurston was working more than partying, however. She earned some money as a waitress, and she focused on her writing. The *Opportunity* contest had elicited more than seven hundred submissions from African-American writers. Zora Hurston hoped hers might be among the best.

The awards banquet was held on May 1, 1925, at a Manhattan restaurant around the corner from the offices of the sponsoring National Urban League. *Opportunity* editor Charles Johnson had raised more than eight hundred dollars in prize money. In addition, he had put together an impressive panel of judges from different fields in the arts.

More than three hundred people attended the dinner. The *New York Herald Tribune* reported the next day: "A novel sight that dinner—white critics, whom everybody knows, Negro writers whom nobody knew—meeting on common ground."[7]

Hurston's work was honored with four prizes
at the *Opportunity* awards dinner.

After the honors were announced, anyone who had not before heard the name Zora Neale Hurston had learned it. Hurston was the winner of four prizes, more than any other entrant. She received significant award money and her first major public recognition.

Among the attendees impressed by Hurston's success that evening was the president of Barnard College, a woman named Annie Nathan Meyer. Barnard is the women's division of Columbia University, the Ivy League school in northern Manhattan not far from Harlem. Before leaving the *Opportunity* dinner, Meyer asked Hurston if she would be interested in attending Barnard.

Hurston had wanted to finish college ever since she had left Howard University. A second chance to do that at Barnard was an exciting prospect. When Meyer told her that she would be the school's only African-American student, Hurston was not troubled; finding the money for tuition was a far greater concern for her.

Meyer was able to arrange some scholarship money immediately and Hurston enrolled at Barnard in September 1925. In a letter to Meyer, Hurston expressed her deep thanks: "I am striving desperately for a toe-hold on the world. You see, your interest keys me up wonderfully—*I must not let you* be disappointed in me."[8]

Hurston's fearlessness at breaking the color line at Barnard was striking. She was grateful to have caught the attention of Annie Nathan Meyer, but she believed at the

Hurston on the campus of Barnard
College in New York City in 1925

same time that she was deserving of the opportunity. She described her mind-set years later, "I had the same feeling at Barnard that I did at Howard, only more so. I felt that I was highly privileged and determined to make the most of it. I did not resolve to be a grind, however, to show the white folks that I had brains. I took it for granted that they knew that."[9]

Midway through her first semester, Hurston was already out of money. The scholarship had gone toward her tuition for classes, but she had also bought school supplies, clothing, and food. She needed a job, and for the second time a woman who had attended the *Opportunity* banquet stepped up to help.

Fannie Hurst was one of the most popular authors in America at that time and a friend of Annie Nathan Meyer. When Meyer wrote to her in Hurston's behalf in October 1925, Hurst offered Hurston a job as her secretary. After classes ended each day, Hurston typed, answered the telephone, and did general errands.

After less than a month, it was clear that Zora Hurston was no secretary. Hurst described it this way: "Her shorthand was short on legibility, her typing hit-or-miss, mostly the latter, her filing a game of find-the-thimble."[10] While Hurston's secretarial stint ended almost as soon as it began, her relationship with Fannie Hurst continued.

Hurst very much enjoyed Hurston's company, describing her as someone with a "blazing zest for life."[11] And she

Hurston was delighted to find that Harlem had a thriving intellectual community. Here, members of a literary club meet at the New York Public Library.

enjoyed the role of mentor, making suggestions for changes to Hurston's stories and promising to bring them to her editors at the publishing house.

For her part, Zora Hurston appreciated Fannie Hurst's stylish flair and celebrity. More shrewdly perhaps, Hurston also recognized the status conferred on her by the friendship. "Partly because you took me under your shelter, I have had no trouble in making friends," she told Hurst later. "Your friendship was a tremendous help to me at a critical time.

It made both faculty and students see me when I needed seeing."[12]

Like Annie Nathan Meyer, Fannie Hurst was interested in encouraging Hurston's ambitions for two reasons. The first was because she believed Hurston was talented. The second was that she believed in supporting African-American culture. Hurston came up with a name for prominent white humanitarians like Meyer, Hurst, and others who championed the black cause: she called them "Negrotarians."

Fortunately for Hurston, she received another scholarship soon after the holiday break. With her immediate money worries solved, Hurston concentrated on her studies. When her faculty adviser suggested a class in anthropology, the study of human culture, Hurston thought it sounded interesting. What she could not have anticipated was how directly this class was going to change her life.

The anthropology department at Columbia, where women from Barnard were welcome to take classes, was world-renowned. Its reputation came largely from the acclaim given to the work of one professor there, Franz Boas.

Boas was the world's expert in an area of anthropology called cultural relativism. Cultural relativists believe that no race is better than another. Instead, each has its own unique characteristics and merits.

An anthropology course
with Professor Franz
Boas changed the course
of Hurston's life.

◆◆◆◆◆

Boas impressed Hurston with his profound intelligence and direct manner. "He wants facts, not guesses," she wrote, "and he can pin you down so expertly that you soon lose the habit of talking all over your face . . . that man can make people work the hardest with just a look or a word, of anybody else in creation."[13]

One of her early assignments for Boas took advantage of Hurston's color and outgoing personality. To challenge the racist notion that blacks had smaller brains than whites, Hurston walked the streets of Harlem asking strangers if she might measure their skulls. It is easy to imagine someone taking offense at this, but by all accounts, Hurston's charm soothed any sore feelings.[14]

For the rest of her time at Barnard, and for some years

after, she studied under Boas, whom she called "the King of Kings."[15] As his student, Hurston learned to appreciate from a different perspective the culture in which she had been raised. Hurston discovered that the proud people of Eatonville were unique and valuable subjects for any anthropologist.

Hurston soon realized that anthropology appealed to her own talents as a writer and a storyteller. Almost ten years later, she would begin the book she wrote on African-American culture with the observation, "It was only when I was off in college, away from my native surroundings, that I could see myself like somebody else and stand off and look at my garment. Then I had to have the spy-glass of Anthropology to look through at that."[16]

Chapter 5

A Godmother's Hand

During their summer break from classes in 1926, Zora Neale Hurston and some of her friends decided to create a literary magazine. They wanted it to be both original and rebellious. Just in case an unsuspecting reader missed the message, they decided to call it *Fire!!*

The contributors to *Fire!!* were young and just making names for themselves. Novelist Wallace Thurman was chosen as editor. Langston Hughes and Countee Cullen signed on to write poetry, Aaron Douglas provided illustrations, and Zora Hurston supplied both a short story called "Sweat" and the play *Color Struck*, for which she had won an award at the *Opportunity* dinner.

The creators of *Fire!!* planned to make it different from rival African-American publications which were sponsored by political organizations. *Opportunity* was produced by the

National Urban League. The National Association for the Advancement of Colored People (NAACP) put out a magazine called *The Crisis*, which had a larger readership than any other.

The Crisis was edited by W.E.B. Du Bois, the foremost African-American intellectual of his day. Twenty years earlier, Du Bois had published a collection of essays called *The Souls of Black Folk*, in which he identified the "color line" as the most pressing problem of the twentieth century. One of the ways blacks might fight bigotry, Du Bois believed, was by creating art that educated its audience about the beauty of the race.

At *Fire!!* the contributors argued, there was to be no

political agenda. Art would be made not as a teaching tool, but for its own sake. The magazine had but one mission; the editor wrote: "We have no axes to grind . . . we are primarily and intensely devoted to art."[1]

W.E.B. Du Bois

Fire!! was originally scheduled to come out four times a year. Instead, the first issue was also its last. At a cost of one dollar, an issue of the magazine was simply too expensive for its intended readers. The magazine cost nearly a thousand dollars to produce. It ended up taking editor Wallace Thurman nearly three years just to pay back the printer. In a strange ending, all the unsold issues ended up burning in an actual office fire.

By the end of the winter term, February 1927, Zora Hurston had accumulated enough credits to graduate from Barnard. But Professor Boas was still hoping to keep one of his favorite students around for a while, so he arranged a six-month research fellowship for Hurston. The money for the grant came from the foundation of the most important African-American historian in the country, a man named Carter G. Woodson.[2] Hurston was asked to collect the stories, songs, and customs of African Americans in the South.

African-American folklore had received almost no scholarly attention until this point. Hurston's work would place her at the forefront of a new field. She told Boas she wanted to begin her research in her hometown. "I hurried back to Eatonville," she wrote, "because I knew that the town was full of material and that I could get it without hurt, harm or danger."[3]

In many regards, Hurston was a natural choice as a researcher for Franz Boas. Raised in the Deep South, she understood it in ways that a northerner never would. Second, Hurston's charm and engaging personality would open doors that stayed closed to another. Finally, a collector of African-American folklore who was African-American herself was far more likely to be welcomed into an African-American setting.

In order to get around, Zora Hurston bought a used car that she nicknamed Sassy Susie. Driving into Eatonville, she spied the usual gathering on the porch of Joe Clark's general store. "I was delighted," she wrote. "The town had not changed. Same love of talk and song."[4]

Yet Hurston soon discovered that collecting folklore was going to be more difficult than she had anticipated. What she had learned from her college textbooks did not help much out in the field. Besides, her university degree got her nowhere with the regular folk of Eatonville.

"The glamour of Barnard College was still upon me," she wrote. "I dwelt in marble halls. I knew where the material was all right. But, I went around asking, in carefully accented Barnardese, 'Pardon me, but do you know any folk tales or folk songs?'"[5]

After nearly three months making the rounds in central Florida without real progress, Hurston sent her first report to Professor Boas. He was not pleased. He reminded Hurston that he was far less interested in the content of a story or song than "the form of diction, movements, and so on."[6] Anyone could use a sound recorder merely to get the words, Boas argued. He wanted Hurston to interpret the style and expression behind them.

In mid-May 1927, Zora Hurston took a break from work. She drove to St. Augustine, Florida, and she married her longtime boyfriend, Herbert Sheen. He had come down to meet her from Chicago, where he was still in medical school. Three days after the ceremony, Hurston wrote friends a happy note, reading in part, "Yes, I'm married now, Mrs. Herbert Arnold Sheen, if you please."[7]

In fact, the two would separate informally by summer's end and divorce four years later. While Hurston told Sheen years after they parted, "your own mother has never loved you to the depth I have," she also admitted she had doubts from the start.[8] The marriage failed because both partners valued their careers more than each other. Hurston confided in friends, "Herbert holds me back . . . he was one of the obstacles that worried me."[9] At a time when marriage was the ultimate goal for most women, Hurston's thoughts and actions were modern ones.

The fact that Zora Hurston could drive a car also made her a daring woman for her day. That, as a black woman, she drove alone in the racist rural South was almost unimaginable. To protect herself, Hurston always carried a pistol in her purse.

In late July 1927, Hurston gained a passenger on her travels. By coincidence, she and her close friend Langston Hughes ended up in Mobile, Alabama, at the same time.

During her travels through Alabama, Zora Hurston, right—
with Langston Hughes, center, and Jessie Fauset—stopped
for this photo in front of a statue honoring Booker T.
Washington, a famous African-American educator.

Hughes thought it would be great fun to accompany Hurston on her research trip.[10] Not being a Southerner himself, he appreciated his friend's familiarity with the surroundings. (Not being a driver, he appreciated her even more!)

For the next month, the two sought folklore in the backwoods of Alabama and Georgia. Hurston believed that her best chance at finding authentic material was to go "where there are the least outside influences and these people, being usually under-privileged, are the shyest."[11]

As writers, both were especially interested in the creative language used by the African Americans they interviewed. Hughes jotted down many expressions he had never heard before. For Hurston, these were the words of her childhood, but it had been a long time since she had heard them spoken.

At the beginning of September 1927, Zora Hurston drove back to New York City. While she had found some useful material on her trip, overall it had not been a success. Hurston was a beginner anthropologist and it showed. While she "cried salty tears" to Professor Boas, he assured her there would be other opportunities for her in the future.[12]

As it happened, opportunity appeared almost immediately, in the unlikely form of an elderly white woman. Her name was Charlotte Van der Veer Quick Osgood Mason. Her family had been wealthy for many generations, and

The Catfish Story from *Mules and Men*

Now take cat-fish for instances. Ah knows a man dat useter go fishin' every Sunday. His wife begged him not to do it and his pastor strained wid him for years but it didn't do no good. He just would go ketch him a fish every Sabbath. One Sunday he went and just as soon as he got to de water he seen a great big ole cat-fish up under some water lilies pickin' his teeth with his fins. So de man baited his pole and dropped de hook right down in front of de big fish. Dat cat grabbed de hook and took out for deep water. De man held on and pretty soon dat fish pulled him in. He couldn't git out. Some folks on de way to church seen him and run down to the water but he was in too deep. So he went down de first time and when he come up he hollered—"Tell my wife." By dat time de fish pulled him under again. When he come up he hollered, "Tell my wife—" and went down again. When he come up de third time he said: "Tell my wife to fear God and cat-fish," and he went down for de last time and he never come up no mo'.[13]

she lived in a fancy apartment on Park Avenue. As a young woman, Mason had lived for a while in the Southwest and studied the music of American Indians. Though she was now in her seventies, she remained actively interested in anthropology.

Mason also was very interested in African-American culture. To that end, she had given tens of thousands of dollars to a number of African-American intellectuals and artists, among them Alain Locke and Langston Hughes. It was Locke, Zora Hurston's mentor at Howard University, who first mentioned Hurston to Mason.[14]

Charlotte Mason and Zora Hurston liked each other immensely on first meeting; so much so, that Hurston believed there was a "psychic bond between us. She could read my mind, not only when I was in her presence, but thousands of miles away."[15]

Mason proposed a business arrangement with Hurston in which she would pay her a yearly salary to collect black folklore. Mason asked that Hurston keep the terms of the agreement and the results of her research secret, and that she call her "Godmother."[16]

When Hurston met Mason she had almost no money left from the Woodson grant. Mason appeared suddenly in her life much like the fairy godmother does for Cinderella. Hurston was to be paid $200 a month, far more than she had ever earned.

Charlotte Mason insisted on being called
"Godmother." She paid expenses for young writers
like Hurston so they could focus on their art.

Everyone whom Mason supported was required to call her Godmother. The name carried a different weight than would have the traditional "Mrs. Mason." As Langston Hughes once said, she "possessed the power to control people's lives—pick them up and put them down when and where she wished."[17]

Charlotte Mason's intelligence, strong will, and dominating personality were alternately charming and frustrating to her patrons. Her generosity was as great as her demands. She was as open-minded as she was arrogant. Mason hired Hurston because she believed in the writer's talents, but only after Hurston agreed not to share any of her research with anyone else.

Ten days before Christmas 1927, Zora Hurston boarded a train for Mobile, Alabama. She planned to interview a man named Cudjo Lewis, the only known survivor of the last slave ship to come to America from Africa.

This was actually the second time Hurston would be interviewing Lewis. She had spoken with him a few months before on her first trip to the South. In fact, Hurston wrote up her interview with Lewis for Professor Boas, copying parts of another journalist's article and citing them as her own.[18] Neither Boas nor anyone else would uncover this plagiarism during her life.

> Ten days before Christmas 1927, Zora Hurston boarded a train for Mobile, Alabama.

It is impossible to know for certain why Hurston cheated. It is likely that she was feeling intense academic pressure and not above doing what made her look smart. Given a second chance, she made Cudjo Lewis the first stop on her trip. It appears that she wanted to set things right.

Just after the New Year, in the new car Charlotte Mason had bought to replace Sassy Susie, Zora Hurston set off on her second folklore-collecting expedition. Peering through what she had called "the spy-glass of anthropology," her immediate future looked very bright.

Chapter 6

High Spirits and Hoodoo

From the start it was obvious to Hurston that her second trip south would prove far more fruitful than her first. When she had finished interviewing Cudjo Lewis, the former slave, she drove five hundred miles east. For the next several months she lived and collected folklore at the Everglades Cypress Lumber Camp in Loughman, Florida.

At the camp, Hurston initiated what she called her "lying contests." A lying contest pitted storytellers against one another. Whoever could tell the tallest tale won a prize. Hurston hung flyers at the post office and company store publicizing the events. "I not only collected a great deal of material," she wrote, "but it started individuals coming to me privately to tell me stories they had no chance to tell during the contest."[1]

Hurston would have stayed longer at the work camp were it not for the scary clash in the jook joint with the knife-wielding Lucy. For some time after, Hurston remembered, "I shivered at the thought of dying with a knife in my back."[2]

After the quick getaway from the turpentine camp, Hurston planned to go to New Orleans. Eatonville was conveniently on the way. Hurston stopped in her home-town to gather her wits and rest awhile. While there, she wrote Langston Hughes: "I am truly dedicated to the work at hand and so I am not even writing, but living every moment with the people. . . . I am getting inside of Negro art and lore. I am beginning to *see* really."[3]

Because Hurston always considered herself a writer first, and a folklorist second, she felt the need to explain herself to her friend. She had put aside her writing for the moment because she had a job. Yet she also recognized that the stories she was being paid to collect would shape her future work. As she added in her letter to Hughes, "Most gorgeous possibilities are showing themselves con-stantly."[4]

But there was something else that kept Zora Hurston from writing, and that was her agreement with Charlotte Mason. By contract, Mason had first dibs on everything Hurston collected. Without Mason's approval, Hurston was prohibited from publishing.

Not everyone might have agreed to this arrangement. But for Hurston, the deal was not such a bad one. Just out of college, she was drawing a decent salary, she had a car, and she rarely had to check in with her boss. In exchange for postponing the publication of her work, she enjoyed responsibility and independence that was rare then for a woman.

Hurston arrived in New Orleans in August 1928. She had chosen this city in southern Louisiana for a particular reason: New Orleans was the center of hoodoo. Hoodoo—or conjure, as it is also called—is a traditional set of beliefs much like a religion.

Hoodoo was created on plantations. Forced by their owners to become Christians, some slaves secretly continued their African traditions. While pretending to adopt the white man's religion, they really practiced something different.

At the core of hoodoo is the belief that a specially trained person, called a conjurer or a hoodoo doctor, can harness spirits to change circumstances. Hoodoo continued to thrive in the years after the end of slavery.

Most often, people turned to hoodoo to cure illness. Conventional medicine was expensive and unfamiliar to many southern African Americans. Hoodoo doctors were trained in the use of traditional African remedies using roots and herbs. Roots were employed to help heal everything from rotting teeth to snakebites to deafness.

A root doctor was not necessarily a hoodoo doctor. Roots had proven medicinal value, and their use was widespread. A hoodoo doctor knew how to use roots and also call on the spiritual world for guidance.

People might also go to a hoodoo doctor if they needed help getting a job or finding romance. Writing a sweetheart's name nine times on a piece of paper and shoving that paper inside a lemon began one ritual for finding love.[5] Following a rash of bad luck, someone might ask the conjurer to use his mojo, a charm that warded off a hex, or curse.

The most famous conjurer in New Orleans had been a

To Make People Love You: A Hoodoo Conjure (from *Mules and Men*)

Take nine lumps of starch, nine of sugar, nine teaspoons of steel dust. Wet it all with Jockey Club cologne. Take nine pieces of ribbon, blue, red, or yellow. Take a dessertspoonful and put it on a piece of ribbon and tie it in a bag. As each fold is gathered together call his name. As you wrap it with yellow thread call his name until you finish. Make nine bags and place them under a rug, behind an armoire, under a step or over a door. They will love you and give you everything they can get. Distance makes no difference. Your mind is talking to his mind and nothing beats that.[6]

woman named Marie Leveau. While Leveau had died almost fifty years earlier, Zora Hurston wanted to meet anyone who had studied under her. She wrote Langston Hughes, "I have landed here in the kingdom of Marie Leveau and expect to wear her crown someday."[7]

It was easy for Hurston to find conjurers who claimed a connection of some kind with the renowned Leveau. It was harder for her to find one who would agree to teach her anything about hoodoo. Just as the slaves had kept hoodoo rituals a secret, so did the later believers.

One good reason for secrecy was that hoodoo was against the law in New Orleans. This had been true since the time of Marie Leveau, who supposedly had once held off the entire city police force by hypnotizing them.[8] To the white Christians in positions of power in Louisiana, hoodoo loomed as a frightening evil magic.[9]

In order to persuade the conjurers to let her in on their secrets, Zora Hurston understood that she first had to convince them of her unbending faith in their traditions. "Mouths don't empty themselves unless the ears are sympathetic and knowing," she wrote.[10]

Hurston spent the next six months living among the hoodoo doctors of New Orleans. As she had done at the turpentine camp in central Florida, she plunged full tilt into their lives. With each conjurer, she began her training with a series of tests, useful as a way of proving her allegiance and educating her at the same time.

These tests were extremely difficult. Only a dedicated researcher would have dared to follow through with them. In one, Hurston had to lie perfectly still and go without food for three days. Her determination so impressed the conjurer that he went so far as to ask her to become his partner.

Hurston had different ambitions, but at the end of her time in New Orleans it is likely that she knew more about hoodoo than any other researcher in the United States.[11] In this second trip to the South, she had become an accomplished folklore collector. She wrote to her former professor, Franz Boas, "I know where to look and how. . . . I know that you understand, and will be pleased with me when I return."[12]

Zora Hurston spent the next half-year alone in a tiny cabin on the Indian River, in east-central Florida. Here she undertook the massive job of organizing her field notes. She sent rough drafts of her research to Charlotte Mason in New York City. She also began working with Langston Hughes on a secret project.

For some time Hurston and Hughes had talked about writing a musical together. They had broached the idea to Charlotte Mason, who was Hughes's patron also. Mason had vetoed the plan but the two writers thought it far too exciting a venture to ignore. Behind Godmother's back, they started outlining scenes and songs.

Hurston demonstrates some poses from a Crow Indian dance in a New York City apartment.

In the autumn of 1929, just before the stock market crashed on Wall Street, Hurston took a working vacation to the island of Nassau in the Bahamas. She had heard a Bahamian band in southern Florida and was enthralled by the music. "Without giving Godmother a chance to object," Hurston said, she got on a boat.[13]

The Caribbean island did not disappoint her. Hurston was awed by its natural beauty and wholly taken by the singing and dancing of its native people. In a month, she stated she had "collected more than a hundred tunes and resolved to make them known to the world."[14]

A deadly hurricane, described by Hurston as "horrible in its intensity and duration," struck the island for five days at the end of September.[15] She confided to Hughes that she "thought once I'd never get back."[16]

When Hurston did return to the United States, she rented an apartment in Westfield, New Jersey, about twenty-five miles outside New York City. Charlotte Mason arranged for her move to New Jersey, as she had done earlier for Langston Hughes. Now that Hurston and Hughes were living in close proximity, their secret plans for the musical switched into high gear.

Of course, Hurston could not ignore her work for Mason. Hughes helped edit the folklore manuscript that Hurston hoped would soon be published as a book. But much of the writers' time now was devoted to the play they had decided to call *Mule Bone*.

A woman named Louise Thompson, whom Charlotte Mason had hired as a typist, helped them with their draft. If Mason had known what her three employees were working on, she would have been very angry. As it happened, what came to pass from this collaboration had even more far-reaching consequences.

Mule Bone was a three-act comedy based on a folk story Hurston had learned as a girl in Eatonville. A musical comedy featuring ordinary African Americans was a novel idea. The infamous minstrel shows—stage productions in which white performers blackened their faces and romanticized the nightmare of slavery—had existed since the end of the Civil War. But a folk comedy showing everyday African-American life would be something new.

Unfortunately, no one would ever get to see *Mule Bone*. The writers began arguing over who should get credit for writing the play and how they might split the proceeds. Then, angry with Hughes over a separate issue, Charlotte Mason cut him from her payroll. The sensitive Hughes was so distraught by this he became ill and went to his mother's home to recover.

During his convalescence, Hughes learned that a famous acting troupe in Cleveland, Ohio, was rehearsing a play by Zora Neale Hurston called *Mule Bone*. Outraged, Hughes immediately called Hurston, demanding an explanation.

Hurston admitted only to having given a copy of the musical to an influential friend in New York. Apparently,

Chapter 7

Folktales

Z ora Hurston and Charlotte Mason did not part
on bad terms. In fact, Mason continued to send
Hurston money while she put the final touches
on the folklore book. Mason's support in 1932
was crucial for Hurston. This was the time of the Great
Depression, a period of severe economic hardship when
one in four Americans were out of work. Black Americans
were losing their jobs at a rate three times that of whites.

Hurston was well aware of the difficulty of finding a
publisher for her book when business everywhere was so
bad. To make some money in the meantime, she contem-
plated opening a small catering business on the side.[1]
When Godmother balked at funding this, Hurston turned
her focus to the stage.

Though her collaboration with Langston Hughes had
failed, Zora Hurston still believed that folklore could make
good theater. To this end, she decided to write and produce
a musical for Broadway. With a cast of fifty-two people, this

For Zora, the most exciting and prolific time
of her life was about to begin.

was a major undertaking for someone with no Broadway experience.

Hurston called her show *The Great Day*. It dramatized a twenty-four-hour period in a workers' camp very much like the one where she had spent time in Florida. The actors told lively stories, sang blues and gospel music, and danced. Hurston asked a famous black choral director for help with the music but he declined, arguing that white audiences would not be interested in black folktales and spirituals.

A Broadway musical is very expensive to produce. Hurston sold her car to help defray some of the many costs but still came up short. Charlotte Mason agreed to lend her enough money to stage the show for a single night at the John Golden Theater on West Fifty-eighth Street.

The musical was a rousing success with the audience and the theater critics. Even the choral director who had earlier refused to help admitted he had been wrong, telling Hurston, "I really came to see you do a flop, but it was swell!"[2]

Yet despite the play's artistic triumph, no financial backers came forward. Without additional support, *The Great Day* could not continue. While the show's immediate closing disappointed Hurston, she was buoyed by the audience's reception. "LET THE PEOPLE SING, was and is my motto," she wrote afterward. "I am satisfied that I proved my point."[3]

Hurston was gratified, but she was also nearly penniless. The small amount she had saved had all gone toward the musical. In a pattern that would repeat itself time and again during difficult times in her life, Hurston yearned for the place of her girlhood. She turned to Godmother for two things: the train fare to Florida and money for new shoes.

Charlotte Mason consented to help, and Hurston left New York as soon as she could manage it. In a letter to Mason written not long after her arrival in Eatonville, she said: "I am happy here, happier than I have been for years. . . . I am renewed like the eagle."[4]

The peace of mind that Eatonville lent Hurston allowed her to begin writing "the novel that I have wanted to write since 1928."[5] This novel had its roots in a short story—a short story that was so good that the famous New York publisher who read it asked Hurston for a book.

This short story was called "The Gilded Six-Bits" and it had just been published in the August 1933 issue of the literary magazine *Story*. It was a tale of love and conflict between a young couple from Eatonville. When Bertram Lippincott, owner of J.B. Lippincott, Inc., one of the most important publishing houses in the country, read "The Gilded Six-Bits," he wrote Hurston asking her if she had a novel he might publish.

While Hurston had been contemplating a novel, she actually had not written a single page of it. But important

Hurston decided to travel back to Eatonville, Florida, where she could write with no distractions.

publishers do not often ask young writers for work. Knowing this, Hurston told Lippincott she would have something for him soon.

For the next three months, Hurston worked tirelessly. In her rented room, she wrote all day at a rickety old table that was the only piece of furniture besides her bed. She stretched the fifty cents her cousin managed to lend her for groceries each week. Hurston borrowed the $2 she needed for postage to get the finished draft to the publisher. And on the day she mailed it, she was evicted from her room for failing to pay the rent.

Yet two weeks later, Bertram Lippincott sent her a very welcome telegram. It offered a two-hundred-dollar advance and contained the exceedingly good news that her book, which she had titled *Jonah's Gourd Vine*, was going to be published by his company. Hurston would write later, "I never expect to have a greater thrill than that wire gave me."[6]

Not only was Zora Hurston desperately in need of the money, the book was the most significant work she had yet published. *Jonah's Gourd Vine* is a story modeled in many ways after Hurston's own life. Its main characters are named John and Lucy, like her parents. The book's folktales and dialogue spring directly from her youth in Eatonville.

The book reviewers liked *Jonah's Gourd Vine* so much that it was selected for the national Book of the Month

Club. Bertram Lippincott liked it so much he agreed to publish Hurston's collection of folklore as well.

She had decided to call this folklore anthology *Mules and Men*. As in *Mule Bone*, the play she had tried to produce with Langston Hughes, Hurston used the mule as a metaphor for slavery. Like slaves, mules are bought and sold. More important, though, mules carry life's burdens with stubborn strength.

Since she had originally written *Mules and Men* as a scholarly book, Lippincott asked her to revise parts of it in order to ensure its appeal to a general audience. Hurston agreed to the revisions but requested that her former professor, Franz Boas, still be asked to write the book's preface.

Mules and Men was slated for publication the following year. In the interim, Hurston was offered a scholarship to do graduate work in anthropology. She was delighted by this turn of events, writing to Boas, "you don't know how I have longed for a chance to stay at Columbia and study."[7] Yet before she began a single class, the funding was withdrawn.

Deeply disappointed but determined to do some anthropology work on her own, Hurston left on a road trip with Alan Lomax. The son of the esteemed folklore collector John Lomax, Alan was a college student who would soon make his own indelible mark as a collector of folksongs.

John and Alan Lomax

John Lomax (1867–1948) and his son Alan (1915–2002) devoted their lives to recording the music and oral histories of the American South. The Lomaxes were most interested in the folklore of ordinary people: cowboys, farmers, ex-slaves, and prisoners were given equal time on their audiotapes. The Lomax Archive of American Folk Song is a collection of more than ten thousand recordings now stored at the Library of Congress.

Hurston and Lomax drove to the Georgia Sea Islands weighed down with the five-hundred-pound recording machine Lomax had on loan from the music division of the Library of Congress. In a week, they had recorded nearly fifty songs. "In the field, Zora was absolutely magnificent!" Lomax related.[8] And in a report to his employer, Lomax credited Hurston as being "probably the best informed person today on Western Negro folk-lore."[9]

At summer's end, Hurston drove to New York City. Though her second book was about to be published, she could find no work as a writer. The year prior, President Franklin Delano Roosevelt had introduced a number of work programs aimed at easing the terrible unemployment that had been brought on by the Depression. These were part of a larger group of programs called the New Deal.

Hurston recorded the stories told by African Americans in the South.

In October 1935, Hurston signed on with one of these programs, a group called the Federal Theater Project. Based in Harlem, the troupe's members were paid a minimal wage to put on plays. For six months, Hurston was employed as a drama coach.

During this same time, *Mules and Men* was finally published. Its seventy folktales and five descriptions of hoodoo illustrated southern African-American folk traditions in a way no author had ever done before. Hurston's careful recording of dialect, the particular regional language the storytellers used, was also new to most readers.

Because *Mules and Men* was such an original book, it drew a mix of responses from reviewers. The famous author and poet Carl Sandburg praised it as "a bold and beautiful book, many a page priceless and unforgettable."[10]

But other readers were more critical. Some African-American scholars protested that Hurston described only the positive parts of African-American culture and ignored the painful racism that affected all aspects of African-American life. The renowned poet Sterling Brown wrote, "*Mules and Men* should be more bitter; it would be nearer the total truth."[11]

Despite this negativity, the publication of *Mules and Men*, following on the heels of *Jonah's Gourd Vine*, pushed Zora Hurston into the national limelight. She was considered to be both a respected authority on African-American folklore and a talented author.

Hurston traveled to the Caribbean,
where she learned about the native cultures.

The success of her two books led Hurston to apply for a grant from the Guggenheim Foundation. Fellowships were awarded only to "men and women who demonstrated exceptional capacity for productive scholarship or exceptional creative ability in the arts."[12]

In March 1936, the Guggenheim Foundation awarded Hurston a yearlong grant to study the folklore practices of blacks in the West Indies. She traveled first to Jamaica, where she lived in the mountains in a remote Maroon settlement. The Maroons are descendants of a warrior group who fought their way out of slavery.

Hurston recorded many of the rituals of the Maroon medicine men and accompanied the group on a wild boar hunt. She also took part in a nine-day funeral rite believed to keep the newly dead from rejoining the living. Thoroughly relishing her experiences, Hurston wrote Guggenheim director Henry Allen Moe that "I am beginning to gather material wholesale here. Just squat down awhile and after that things begin to happen."[13]

After six months in Jamaica, Hurston took a boat to Haiti. In the capital city of Port-au-Prince, she rented a small house. Immediately, she became aware that the hoodoo she had observed in New Orleans was nothing compared to what was

> She traveled first to Jamaica, where she lived in the mountains in a remote Maroon settlement.

practiced in Haiti. These intense practices outside the United States were referred to as voodoo.

In Haiti, Hurston found a type of voodoo she called "both beautiful and terrifying."[14] She witnessed séances (attempts to communicate with the dead), animal sacrifices, and a funeral ceremony in which the corpse "sat up with its staring eyes, bowed its head and fell back again."[15] Her "greatest thrill was coming face to face with a zombie and photographing her."[16] (A zombie is a corpse that appears to have come back to life.)

For Hurston, Haiti was also a place of singular beauty, providing "a peace I have never known anywhere else on earth."[17] It was here, in the last seven weeks of 1936, that she feverishly wrote her second novel, the book for which she would receive her greatest acclaim.

Chapter 8

Love Stories

The book that Zora Hurston wrote in Haiti was a heated tale of love and passion. One of the reasons she was able to write it as quickly as she did was that the story drew directly from her own life. Hurston's trip to the West Indies was foremost a prestigious Guggenheim-financed research expedition. But it was something else also: It was an escape from the tangled ends of a difficult relationship.

As Hurston put it most colorfully, "I did not just fall in love. I made a parachute jump."[1] The man's name was Percival McGuire Punter. Born in 1912, he was more than twenty years younger than Hurston, handsome and intelligent. Hurston had first noticed him when he sang in the Broadway show she produced.

For Hurston, this was "the real love affair of my life."[2] She described Punter as "so extraordinary that I lived in terrible fear lest women camp on his doorstep in droves and take him away from me."[3]

Yet when he insisted Hurston give up her career, the relationship faltered. "I really wanted to do anything he wanted me to do, but that one thing I could not do," she said later.[4] To dodge her pained heart, Hurston fled to the Caribbean. There she threw herself full force into the very work Punter wanted to deny her.

Zora Hurston called her love story *Their Eyes Were Watching God*. Its central characters, Janie Crawford and Tea Cake, are fictional versions of Hurston and Punter. Under extreme conditions—including a violent hurricane and a rabid dog—Janie demonstrates the resourcefulness and independence that Hurston clearly valued in her own life.

As in her earlier books, the characters express themselves in the rich dialect of Eatonville. Like the residents of that town, they gather on each other's front porches to tell stories. In the end, *Their Eyes Were Watching God* is revealed as one long porch tale Janie Crawford relates to a friend.

In 1937, Lippincott published *Their Eyes Were Watching God* to solid reviews. One newspaper columnist likened Hurston to the famed English author, D. H. Lawrence.[5] But as had been the case with *Mules and Men*, Hurston's reception among African-American writers and thinkers was far less positive.

Richard Wright, who would later become known for his books *Black Boy* and *Native Son*, dismissed Hurston in

Richard Wright was highly critical of Hurston's work.

the magazine *New Masses*. Her work had no backbone, he contended, "no theme, no message, no thought."[6] By "no message," Wright meant no obvious political message. He believed that African-American writers in America had a responsibility to protest racism. Wright even compared the characters in *Their Eyes Were Watching God* to actors in a minstrel show.[7]

In a review for *Opportunity*, Alain Locke also was very tough on his former pupil. He began by admiring Hurston's "gift for poetic phrase, for rare dialect, and folk humor."[8] He went so far as to say it was "folklore fiction at its best."[9] Then Locke switched to sharp criticism. To his mind, folklore was not fiction worth taking seriously.[10]

While Richard Wright's criticism was stinging, Zora Hurston was furious at Alain Locke. She immediately wrote a letter to *Opportunity* that the editors refused to publish. She said, in typically vivid Hurston fashion: "I will send my toenails to debate him on what he knows about Negroes and Negro life, and I will come personally to debate him on what he knows about literature on the subject."[11]

What particularly angered Hurston as an author was being told what to write. *Their Eyes Were Watching God* was her book, not Locke's, and Hurston passionately believed in the merits of folklore. What particularly incensed her as an African American was his suggestion that her down-home characters were any less noble for being content with their lot.

After the promotion tour for her novel was over, Hurston left New York City to return to Haiti as the recipient of a second Guggenheim fellowship. She intended to write a full-length book on the subject of voodoo.

The research was progressing well until one night about a month after her arrival. In an isolated part of the jungle, Hurston suddenly became deathly ill. In a letter to Henry Allen Moe, the Guggenheim director, she typed in all capital letters: "I HAVE HAD A VIOLENT GAS-TRIC DISTURBANCE."[12]

Hurston believed the cause of her severe attack was poison. Against the advice of friends on the island who warned her that "some things were good to know and some things were not," Zora Hurston had bravely pursued some voodoo doctors of dubious reputation.[13]

Hurston had been shown how to make poison by these "bocors," or devil worshippers. Now she supposed that she had become a victim of their methods herself.[14] "For a whole day and night," she wrote Henry Moe, "I'd thought I'd never make it."[15]

As soon as she was able to travel, Hurston returned to the United States to recover and finish writing the book on voodoo. *Tell My Horse* was published in 1938. Most reviews were mixed, but the columnist for the *New York Herald*

The covers of Hurston's books helped convey the rich cultural text inside.

Tribune was so enthusiastic that he suggested Hurston write five more books on the subject.[16]

For the next eighteen months, Hurston earned her living from another of Roosevelt's New Deal work programs. This time she joined the Federal Writers' Project in Jacksonville, Florida. Hurston was hired to research black culture in the state for a book to be called *The Florida Negro*.

Hurston hit the road for weeks on end, gathering material for the book. Her employer there recalled receiving regular reports from her "of the most fabulous folk stuff imaginable. We cared not a whit where and when she collected it, but hastened to sprinkle it about in *The Florida Negro* manuscript for seasoning."[17]

During her stint in Jacksonville, Zora Hurston met a fellow worker named Albert Price, III. He was twenty-three and still in college. Though she was actually forty-eight, Hurston told Price she was twenty-nine. At the end of June 1939, they married.

After only six weeks, Hurston left Price. She complained that he expected her to pay for his schooling and to live with his mother. Clearly, this second marriage fared even worse than Hurston's first.

She packed up her few belongings and took off in a red convertible. Hurston had been offered a teaching job at North Carolina College for Negroes in Durham. One of her responsibilities was to start up a drama department for the school.

From the start, Hurston and the school's president did not see eye to eye. He wanted a teacher who quietly followed his lead. Zora Hurston was never going to be that teacher. She told her students, "We are going to try to make Negro plays out of Negro life in the Negro manner. We are going to have to struggle against people who think if we don't do something highbrow we haven't accomplished anything."[18]

Hurston worked for the Federal Writers' Project
in Jacksonville researching black culture.

By March 1940, Hurston had resigned from her post at the college. She was tired of being told what to do, and she had just published a new book that the *New York Times Book Review* called "literature in every best sense of the word."[19]

Moses, Man of Mountain is different from Hurston's other books. Instead of drawing inspiration from Eatonville, this book retells the biblical story of Moses. In the form of a long fable, Hurston fashions a strong parallel between the enslaved Israelites and the African American experience.

Soon after the book came out, Hurston began a new job with the internationally renowned anthropologists Margaret Mead and Jane Belo. They were studying religious behavior among the Gullah people of coastal South Carolina, descendants of enslaved West Africans.

Hurston met Belo in Beaufort, South Carolina, and the two women began attending church services in the area. With a camera and

◆◆◆◆◆◆◆◆◆◆
Margaret Mead

Margaret Mead (1901–1978) was a noted anthropologist and writer who researched the native peoples of New Guinea, Bali, Samoa, and North America. As Zora Hurston would do just a few years after her, Mead studied under Franz Boas at Barnard College. Mead's focus as an anthropologist was in documenting cultures that had little contact with the modern world. Mead was a pioneer in applying the then-new theories of psychology to understanding culture. Jane Belo was a graduate student who worked under Mead.

an audio device similar to the one she had used with Alan Lomax, Hurston made many recordings of church music and practices. In one such recording, Hurston herself plays the conga drum on a riverbank.[20]

Zora Hurston and Jane Belo became close friends and ardent mutual admirers. Hurston addressed letters to "Jane, the Incomparable," and Belo told colleagues, "We got some perfectly grand stuff in a very short time thanks to Zora's high-spirited and accomplished cooperation."[21]

For some time, Bertram Lippincott had been urging Hurston to write her autobiography. Hurston had believed the idea premature, but Lippincott assured her that a second volume could be produced later in her career. So in the spring of 1941, after she had finished her work with Jane Belo, Zora Hurston went to live as the guest of a friend in southern California.

For the next year, she wrote the autobiography and worked as a writer for Paramount Studios in Hollywood. The studio paid her one hundred dollars a week, the highest salary Hurston ever earned.

Zora Hurston's autobiography, *Dust Tracks on a Road*, was released in November 1942. While much of it relates intimate moments in her life, particularly during her early childhood, more is left out. As Hurston admitted, "I did not want to write it at all, because it is too hard to reveal one's inner self."[22]

Zora had many new experiences as a
folklorist. Here, she beats a drum used
in some religious ceremonies.

Yet with excellent critical reviews, at least in the mainstream press, the book sold very well. Black reviewers continued to disparage Hurston, suggesting in this instance that she had written to please a white audience. Prominent African-American author and critic Arna Bontemps wrote, "Miss Hurston deals very simply with the more serious aspects of Negro life in America—she ignores them."[23]

Despite this jab, *Dust Tracks on a Road* won a prestigious one-thousand-dollar award from the *Saturday Review* for the book's contribution to "the field of race relations."[24] And sometime-friend-sometime-enemy Alain Locke sent a congratulatory letter, pleasing Hurston immensely.[25]

At this point in her career, having published two books on folklore, three novels, an autobiography, and numerous magazine and newspaper articles, Zora Neale Hurston had earned the reputation of a nationally acclaimed African-American author.

In February 1943, this hard-won reputation took a hit. The *New York World-Telegram* quoted Hurston as saying, "The lot of the Negro is much better in the South than the North . . . for everything put up in the South for white people there is the equivalent for the Negro. In other words, the Jim Crow system works."[26]

Hurston was horrified by the *Telegram* article, calling it "untrue and twisted," and adding, "I categorically deny

Hurston's work portrayed African Americans
in the South in a realistic way.

that I ever said that Negroes are better off in the South. Neither did I approve of segregation in the South or anywhere else."[27]

Roy Wilkins of the National Association for the Advancement of Colored People (NAACP) voiced his organization's outrage. Perhaps Hurston was merely spouting words in a publicity stunt, he conjectured. But "now is no time for tongue-wagging by Negroes for the sake of publicity. The race is fighting a battle that may determine its status for fifty years. Those who are not for us, are against us."[28]

While Hurston did not reply directly to the NAACP attack, she published an essay in the *Negro Digest* that clarified her views. "I am all for the repeal of every Jim Crow law in the nation here and now," she began. "Not in another generation or so. The Hurstons have already been waiting 80 years for that." She then concluded, "I give my hand, my heart and my head to the total struggle."[29]

With part of the award money she had won for her autobiography, Hurston bought a house—and not just any house. With characteristic flair, she purchased a thirty-two-foot houseboat. It was twenty years old and badly in need of paint, but Hurston named it the *Wanago* (as in "want to go") and moored it in Daytona Beach, Florida.

On January 18, 1944, Hurston

> "I give my hand, my heart and my head to the total struggle."

married for a third time. James Howell Pitts, a businessman from Ohio, was forty-five, closer to Hurston's fifty-three years, but she claimed to be only forty on their marriage certificate. While the age gap was smaller this time around, the marriage was no more successful. Only eight months later, Hurston and Pitts divorced.

Whatever the reasons for the breakup of this marriage, Hurston was not dejected. In a letter at this time to Henry Allen Moe at the Guggenheim Foundation, she wrote, "the various natural expressions of the day on the river keep me happier than I have ever been before in my life."[30]

Chapter 9

Last Word

Zora Hurston was so content on her river house-boat that only a real adventure could lure her away. This adventure unexpectedly showed up one day in the person of Reginald Brett, a gold miner from Honduras. Brett had read *Tell My Horse*, the book about voodoo in Haiti, and believed Hurston would be very interested in what he had to tell her.

Brett described for Hurston the ruins of an ancient Mayan city. No one outside Honduras had ever seen this city, he explained. It was deep in the jungle and amazingly rich with folklore materials.

When Reginald Brett finished his tale, Hurston felt "like a mule in a tin stable, pitching and rearing and kicking at the walls."[1] Somehow she would have to figure out a way to see this secret lost city. As always, finding the money to do it would prove a big obstacle.

Hurston appealed immediately to the people she knew at the Guggenheim Foundation, but having assisted her with two prior fellowships they said they could do no more. Hurston then sold her car and made a deal with a charter-boat captain: She would pay for provisions and a new paint job for his ship, and he agreed to take her on his sailboat for free.

While she waited for the additional funds necessary to make the trip, Hurston finished up a new novel. But for the first time, Bertram Lippincott decided that he did not think the manuscript was good enough to publish.

Needing another source of income, Zora Hurston sold her beloved houseboat and left Florida for a job in New York City. A politician running for office in Harlem had hired her to help with his campaign.

Hurston stayed in Harlem after the November 1946 elections, scraping out a living writing articles for magazines and newspapers. The following spring her fortunes improved: She found a new publisher—Charles Scribner's Sons—and a new book deal.

The deal for her next novel included an advance of five hundred dollars. With this money, Hurston did what she had been longing to do for nearly two years. She paid for her trip to Honduras.

On May 4, 1947, Hurston sailed to the Honduran island she had been warned was the dangerous habitat of snakes, pumas, jaguars, and hostile Indians.[2] The charter-boat captain with whom she had originally arranged to travel was unavailable at this time, so Hurston booked passage on an ocean liner instead.

For the first months after her arrival, Hurston took a room in a coastal hotel. She wanted to acclimate herself to the area before attempting the arduous trek into the jungle. She also had to finish the manuscript for which she had received the advance money from her new publisher.

Honduras was a special place for Hurston. She confided to her editor, "it has given me back myself. I am my old brash self again."[3] Even the long rainy season did not bother her. "Another month of this weather," she joked to a friend, "and I will be waving you a greeting with a fin."[4]

When she had been away nearly a year, her publisher asked her to return to New York for a while. Her first new work of fiction in almost ten years was being readied for publication. The story of a white family, *Seraph on the Suwanee*, was unlike any other story Hurston had written.

Just as the promotional tour for the new book was being launched, Hurston received the shocking news that she had been charged with molesting a young boy. Her accuser was a former landlady. Hurston had once suggested that the woman's son might benefit from being tested for psychiatric problems.

The charges against Hurston were completely baseless. Hurston's passport proved that she had been in Honduras at the time the alleged abuse was supposed to have taken place. Plainly, the landlady had been angry at Hurston for recommending psychiatric help for her child and had made up the horrendous story.

Still, the ordeal took a terrible toll on Hurston. As she told a close friend, "This thing is too fantastic, too evil, too far from reality for me to conceive of it."[5] The African-American press was particularly hard on her. Several African-American-owned newspapers wrote stories that seemed to convict Hurston in spite of her proven innocence.[6]

Fortunately, the charges largely went unreported in the country's key white-owned papers. This helped sales of *Seraph on the Suwanee*, which, despite generally mediocre reviews, sold very well. Some of the reviews were quite enthusiastic. The *New York Herald Tribune* paid tribute to "Miss Hurston's astonishing, bewildering talent."[7]

As had been the case many times before, Florida provided Hurston with a place of solace. After the nightmarish events in New York, she retreated to Miami, where her friend the charter-boat captain offered her a place to stay on his boat.

The two discussed plans to sail to Honduras together in the near future. Hurston had not been able to get to the ancient Mayan city during her previous visit and was anxious to return. When the charter boat was hired out, Hurston rented a houseboat nearby. She needed a job to pay her rent and she took one that ended up making headlines.

Hurston became cook and maid to a wealthy white family. When the woman who hired her happened to come upon a story Hurston had written in the *Saturday Evening Post*, she was stunned. She had had no idea that her maid was an accomplished author.

Not adverse to a little publicity, Hurston's employer alerted the newspapers to her find. The national wire services immediately spread the word. Too proud to admit she had taken the position because she needed the thirty-dollar-a-week pay, Hurston first claimed she was researching domestic work for a magazine.

She told another interviewer that she was merely taking a break from her writing. "A writer has to stop writing every now and then and just live a little,"[8] she asserted. Of course the truth was something else: Hurston needed the money and she did not consider the labor beneath her. As a young woman, she had worked for close to a decade doing the very same thing.

In the end, all the media hype boosted sales of *Seraph on the Suwanee* and also brought Hurston enough freelance writing work that she was able to quit the maid's job.

Though the public still believed she was much younger, Zora Hurston was then sixty years old. What she craved most at this time was a home of her own. She confided to a friend, "Being under my own roof, and my personality not invaded by others makes a lot of difference in my outlook on life and everything. Oh, to be once more alone in a house!"[9]

By early summer 1951, Hurston had cobbled together enough checks from small writing jobs to rent the same one-room house she had lived in when she wrote *Mules and Men*. The house needed work but Hurston liked doing it, declaring, "I am up every morning at five o'clock chopping down weeds and planting flowers and things. . . . I go to bed happily tired."[10]

While even the five-dollar-a-week rent was a stretch for her, Hurston finally felt like she had come home. She grew her own fruit and vegetables and she caught fish. As she told her editor, "Living the kind of life for which I was made, strenuous and close to the soil, I am happier than I have been for at least ten years."[11]

Zora Hurston lived in her tiny home on the river in Eau Gallie, Florida, for the next five years. Despite recurring health problems, chief among them severe headaches and stomach pains, this would be one of the most comfortable times in her life.

One of the jobs she took during this period was covering a murder trial for the *Pittsburgh Courier*. A black woman named Ruby McCollum had been charged with killing a white doctor. The facts of the case made good copy, especially with Hurston doing the writing.

Ruby McCollum was the wealthiest African-American woman in town and also the longtime mistress of the doctor. When she was arrested for his murder, her husband tried to flee a raging white mob, only to suffer a fatal heart attack.

The evidence supported McCollum's plea of self-defense but an all-white jury sentenced her to die in the electric chair anyway. For six months during and after the trial, Zora Hurston's eloquent stories ran in the *Courier* and provoked an outpouring of letters from readers.

Following McCollum's conviction, Hurston and another journalist were instrumental in getting the case heard on appeal. Before the Florida Supreme Court, Ruby McCollum was declared insane instead and committed to a mental institution. Without question, Zora Hurston helped save her life.

Hurston's other significant writing project of these years was a historical biography of King Herod, the first-century-B.C. ruler. Hurston had been doing research on and off for nearly eight years by this time and was very enthusiastic about her subject matter, claiming, "it is a whale of a story."[12] Unfortunately, her publisher did not see it the same way and rejected the manuscript for *Herod The Great*.

On August 11, 1955, Zora Hurston wrote a letter to the editor of the *Orlando Sentinel* that kicked off a storm of protest. She made public her dislike of *Brown* v. *Board of Education*, the 1954 Supreme Court ruling which outlawed school segregation.

As someone raised in the embracing arms of Eatonville, Florida, Hurston thought an all-African-American school had its merits. "If there are adequate Negro schools and prepared instructors and instructions," she explained in her letter, "then there is nothing different except the presence of white people. For this reason, I find the U.S. Supreme Court as insulting rather than honoring my race."[13]

Of course the obvious problem with Hurston's argument was the near-absence of decent African-American schools outside of rare places like Eatonville. Predictably,

Alice Walker, describing her reaction upon first reading Zora Neale Hurston:
Having found *that Zora* (like a golden key to a storehouse of varied treasure), I was hooked. What I had discovered, of course, was a model. A model, who, as it happened, provided more than voodoo for my story, more than one of the greatest novels America had produced—though, being America, it did not realize this. She had provided, as if she knew someday I would come along wandering in the wilderness, a nearly complete record of her life. And though her life sprouted an occasional wart, I am eternally grateful for that life, warts and all.[14]

Alice Walker renewed public interest in Zora Hurston's writings.

civil rights leaders criticized her comments and white segregationists applauded them loudly.

While Hurston's position may have been unusual for an African American at the time, it was consistent with her outlook on the world. "The whole matter revolves around the self-respect of my people," she wrote. "How much satisfaction can I get from a court order for somebody to associate with me who does not wish me near them?"[15]

In the spring of 1956, to what she called her "terrible distress," the sixty-five-year-old Hurston was forced to move from the home she loved so dearly.[16] The landlord had sold the house and it was no longer available for Hurston to rent.

Hurston moved into a trailer home on Merritt Island, about twenty miles from where she had lived in Eau Gallie. She took a job as a librarian at Patrick Air Force Base. A year later she was fired for being "too well educated for the job."[17]

During her last few years, Hurston suffered greatly from the effects of poor health and poverty. On January 28, 1960, she died of a stroke at Fort Pierce Memorial Hospital. She was sixty-nine years old.

Zora Hurston was buried in an unmarked grave, but the many attendees at her funeral made clear that she died a much-loved person. In

> A year later she was fired for being "too well educated for the job."

1973, Alice Walker, the future author of *The Color Purple*, went to pay her respects at Hurston's grave and found it in total disrepair. In homage to the writer who had most inspired her, Walker had a headstone made in Hurston's memory. Its epitaph was simple and fitting: "Zora Neale Hurston: A Genius of the South."[18]

Chapter 10

Loyal to the Language

Writers and artists of the Harlem Renaissance broke new ground with work that celebrated African-American culture. While Zora Neale Hurston very much belonged to this artistic community, she cannot exactly be defined by it either.

For one thing, while Hurston began writing in the 1920s, she did her best work in the decade following. But the far more important reasons why Hurston was not really a Harlem Renaissance writer have much more to do with the unique person she was and the unique perspective she brought to her writing.

The leading African-American writers in Harlem were inspired by big cities like New York and Paris. Hurston drew instead on her youth in the rural South. The adult conversations she remembered hearing on the front porches of Eatonville, Florida, shaped the core of all her work.

Hurston wrote about southern African Americans using their own rich, idiomatic language. She was never interested in standard grammar and never worried about sounding unrefined. Hurston's characters were literary versions of the proud, self-governing people of Eatonville. If their talk sounded odd to white ears or black intellectuals, Hurston believed, so be it.

Many of the foremost African-American thinkers of Hurston's day did not support her. They believed her use of African-American dialect went against their efforts to bolster their race. Some even went so far as to suggest Hurston's characters encouraged racism.

But Hurston knew otherwise. She cherished the African-American speech of her people. As an anthropologist and as a writer, she understood that the jokes, songs, and stories she wanted to pass on needed to be reported exactly as she heard them. Anything less would misrepresent or dilute their distinctive sound.

Hurston was never oblivious to racism and bore the brunt of its ugliness many times in her life. But because she saw black people as having a culture as full and complex as that of white people, she sought not to hide the differences between the races but rather to celebrate them.

Just as she insisted her characters be true to themselves, Hurston was never afraid to be herself either. She was a bold and independent woman, willing to go anywhere in the world for her work. She traveled alone throughout the Deep South and in the remote jungles of the Caribbean and Central America. She crossed the color line at Barnard College and she ended three marriages when she felt the relationships restricted her work.

Hurston published four novels, two books on folklore, an autobiography, and more than fifty other essays, plays, and short stories. Yet when she died, not a single one of her books was still in print. Despite the great respect she earned for her writing, Hurston always struggled to make a living from it.

She faced real poverty her entire life. Forced to leave school and find a job while just a teen, Hurston worked until the day she died but never had any savings. Though she was courageous and accepting of her circumstances, her life would have been very different without the constant need to worry about money.

Her studies in anthropology placed her among the top scholars in the world in the field of African-American folklore. Her work played a vital role in preserving the cultural heritage of southern African Americans, and *Mules and Men* is still considered one of the very best books on the subject.

But Zora Neale Hurston always considered herself a writer first and folklorist second. In her autobiography, she describes, "the force from somewhere in Space which

Hurston's life and work were vital in preserving
the folklore and the culture of the south.

commands you to write in the first place, gives you no choice. You take up the pen when you are told, and write what is commanded. There is no agony like bearing an untold story inside you."[1]

In the decades since her death, Zora Hurston's books have come back into print and have been translated into seven languages. *Their Eyes Were Watching God*, widely considered her masterwork, has sold more than a million

Hurston's play *Polk County* was rediscovered years after it was written. Here, members of the cast rehearse in 2002.

copies. The Zora Neale Hurston Festival of the Arts and Humanities is a popular event held each year in Eatonville.

Some of the best literature written today, including the books of Alice Walker and Nobel-laureate Toni Morrison, owes a great debt to Zora Neale Hurston. While Hurston's celebratory ways of writing about African-American culture may seem more usual to readers now, they were nothing short of revolutionary when they were written a generation ago.

Chronology

1891—Zora Neale Hurston is born in Notasulga, Alabama, on January 7.

1892—The Hurston family moves to Eatonville, Florida.

1904—Lucy Potts Hurston dies.

1905—John Hurston remarries; Zora is sent to boarding school.

1907—Forced to leave school, she begins eight years at domestic jobs.

1916—Is employed by an acting troupe.

1917—Reenters high school in Baltimore, taking ten years off her actual age.

1919—Father, John Hurston, is killed in automobile accident; Zora graduates from high school; moves to Washington, D.C., to attend Howard University.

1925—Moves to New York City; wins *Opportunity* awards; meets Annie Nathan Meyer and Fannie Hurst; enters Barnard College.

1926—Begins work with anthropologist Franz Boas; produces magazine *Fire!!*

1927—Wins Carter G. Woodson grant to take folklore trip to the South; marries Herbert Sheen; travels with Langston Hughes; works for Charlotte Mason.

1928—Separates from Sheen; continues folklore expedition in Florida and studies hoodoo in New Orleans.

1929—Works on folklore manuscript; travels to the Bahamas and experiences a hurricane.

1930—Moves to Westfield, New Jersey, and works on a musical with Hughes.

1931—Friendship with Hughes ends and contract with Mason ends.

1933—*The Great Day* is produced in New York City; short story "The Gilded Six-Bits" attracts publisher J. B. Lippincott; writes *Jonah's Gourd Vine*; begins love affair with Percival Punter.

1934—*Jonah's Gourd Vine* is published.

1935—Takes work as a drama coach; *Mules and Men* is published.

1936—Receives Guggenheim fellowship; goes to Jamaica, then Haiti; writes *Their Eyes Were Watching God*.

1937—Returns to the United States; begins writing *Tell My Horse*; masterpiece, *Their Eyes Were Watching God*, is published.

1938—Works on Florida folklore project; *Tell My Horse* is published.

1939—Takes job as drama professor; marries Albert Price.

1940—*Moses, Man of Mountain* is published; works with Jane Belo.

CHRONOLOGY

1941—Moves to California to write autobiography and work at Paramount.

1942—Autobiography *Dust Tracks on a Road* is published.

1943—Purchases houseboat.

1944—Marries James Pitts; plans trip to Honduras.

1945—J. B. Lippincott rejects a manuscript.

1946—Works on political campaign in Harlem.

1947—Switches publisher to Scribner's; advance for *Seraph on the Suwanee* finances Honduras trip.

1948—Fights child-abuse charges; *Seraph* is published.

1949—Abuse charges dropped; lives on charter boat in Florida.

1950—Takes maid's job and is discovered by national press.

1951—Moves to one-room house in Eau Gallie; reports on McCollum trial.

1952—Works on biography of Herod.

1956—Leaves home and takes job as a librarian.

1957—Moves to trailer home.

1960—Dies of a stroke on January 28.

Chapter Notes

Chapter 1. **Narrow Escape**

1. Robert Hemenway, *Zora Neale Hurston: A Literary Biography* (Urbana, Ill.: University of Illinois Press, 1980), p. 111.

2. Valerie Boyd, *Wrapped in Rainbows: The Life of Zora Neale Hurston* (New York: Scribner, 2003), p. 157.

3. Zora Neale Hurston, *Dust Tracks on a Road* (New York: HarperPerennial, 1996), p. 154.

4. Ibid., p. 156.

Chapter 2. **Eatonville's Girl**

1. Mary E. Lyons, *Sorrow's Kitchen: The Life and Folklore of Zora Neale Hurston* (New York: Simon & Schuster, 1990), p. 6.

2. Lucy Anne Hurston, *Speak, So You Can Speak Again: The Life of Zora Neale Hurston* (New York: Doubleday, 2004), p. 8.

3. Zora Neale Hurston, *Dust Tracks on a Road* (New York: HarperPerennial, 1996), p. 34.

4. Lyons, p. 13.

5. Hurston, *Dust Tracks*, p. 46.

6. Ibid., p. 47.

7. Valerie Boyd, *Wrapped in Rainbows: The Life of Zora Neale Hurston* (New York: Scribner, 2003), p. 38.

8. Hurston, *Dust Tracks*, pp. 42–43.

9. Boyd, p. 40.

10. Ibid., p. 32.

11. Lyons, p. 4.

12. Hurston, *Dust Tracks*, p. 14.

13. Ibid., p. 66.

14. Boyd, p. 50.

15. Hurston, *Dust Tracks*, p. 85.

Chapter 3. Second Chance

1. Zora Neale Hurston, *Dust Tracks on a Road* (New York: Harper Perennial, 1996), p. 87.

2. Ibid.

3. Ibid., pp. 88–89.

4. Ibid., p. 97.

5. Ibid., p. 105.

6. Valerie Boyd, *Wrapped in Rainbows: The Life of Zora Neale Hurston* (New York: Scribner, 2003), p. 75.

7. Hurston, *Dust Tracks*, p. 126.

8. Ibid., p. 129.

9. Zora Neale Hurston, "John Redding Goes to Sea," *The Stylus Magazine*, Howard University, May 1921.

10. Hurston, *Dust Tracks*, p. 204.

11. Ibid., p. 138.

12. Robert Hemenway, *Zora Neale Hurston: A Literary Biography* (Urbana, Ill.: University of Illinois Press, 1980), p. 9.

Chapter 4. Opportunity Knocks

1. Robert Hemenway, *Zora Neale Hurston: A Literary Biography* (Urbana, Ill.: University of Illinois Press, 1980), p. 29.

2. Steven Watson, *The Harlem Renaissance: Hub of African-American Culture, 1920–1930* (New York: Pantheon Books, 1995): Hughes, p. 50; Bontemps, p. 66; Locke, p. 3; Johnson, p. 158; Ellington, p. 8.

3. Ibid., p. 130.

4. Ibid., p. 131.

5. Ibid.

6. Valerie Boyd, *Wrapped in Rainbows: The Life of Zora Neale Hurston* (New York: Scribner, 2003), p. 95.

7. Watson, p. 66.

8. Carla Kaplan. *Zora Neale Hurston: A Life in Letters* (New York: Doubleday, 2002), p. 55.

9. Zora Neale Hurston, *Dust Tracks on a Road* (New York: Harper Perennial, 1996), p. 140.

10. Boyd, p. 107.

11. Ibid.

12. Ibid., pp. 108–109.

13. Hurston, p. 140.

14. Boyd, p. 114.

15. Hurston, p. 140.

16. Zora Neale Hurston, *Mules and Men* (New York: HarperPerennial, 1990), p. 1.

CHAPTER NOTES

Chapter 5. A Godmother's Hand

1. Valerie Boyd, *Wrapped in Rainbows: The Life of Zora Neale Hurston* (New York: Scribner, 2003), p. 134.

2. Robert E. Hemenway, *Zora Neale Hurston: A Literary Biography* (Urbana, Ill.: University of Illinois Press, 1980), p. 84.

3. Zora Neale Hurston, *Mules and Men* (New York: HarperPerennial, 1990), p. 2.

4. Ibid., p. 7.

5. Zora Neale Hurston, *Dust Tracks on a Road* (New York: HarperPerennial, 1996), pp. 143–144.

6. Hemenway, p. 91.

7. Carla Kaplan, Zora *Neale Hurston: A Life in Letters* (New York: Doubleday, 2002), p. 101.

8. Hemenway, p. 94.

9. Ibid.

10. Boyd, p. 151.

11. Hurston, *Mules and Men*, p. 2.

12. Hurston, *Dust Tracks*, p. 144.

13. Ibid., p. 95.

14. Boyd, p. 156.

15. Hurston, *Dust Tracks*, p. 144.

16. Boyd, pp. 158–159.

17. Ibid., p. 158.

18. Hemenway, pp. 96–97.

Chapter 6. High Spirits and Hoodoo

1. Zora Neale Hurston, *Mules and Men* (New York: HarperPerennial, 1990), p. 65.

2. Ibid., p. 154.

3. Robert Hemenway, *Zora Neale Hurston: A Literary Biography* (Urbana, Ill.: University of Illinois Press, 1980), p. 112.

4. Ibid.

5. Hurston, p. 188.

6. Ibid., p. 276.

7. Carla Kaplan, *Zora Neale Hurston: A Life in Letters* (New York: Doubleday, 2002), p. 124.

8. Hemenway, p. 120.

9. Hurston, p. 185.

10. Ibid.

11. Valerie Boyd, *Wrapped in Rainbows: The Life of Zora Neale Hurston* (New York: Scribner, 2003), p. 182.

12. Ibid., p. 183.

13. Zora Neale Hurston, *Dust Tracks on a Road* (New York: HarperPerennial, 1996), p. 157.

14. Ibid., p. 158.

15. Ibid., p. 159.

16. Kaplan, p. 148.

17. Ibid., p. 202.

18. Ibid.

Chapter 7. Folktales

1. Robert Hemenway, *Zora Neale Hurston: A Literary Biography* (Urbana, Ill.: University of Illinois Press, 1980), p. 161.

2. Valerie Boyd, *Wrapped in Rainbows: The Life of Zora Neale Hurston* (New York: Scribner, 2003), p. 231.

CHAPTER NOTES

3. Zora Neale Hurston, *Dust Tracks on a Road* (New York: HarperPerennial, 1996), p. 172.

4. Carla Kaplan, *Zora Neale Hurston: A Life In Letters* (New York: Doubleday, 2002), p. 254.

5. Ibid.

6. Hurston, p. 175.

7. Hemenway, p. 208.

8. Stetson Kennedy, "What Alan Lomax Meant to Me and This World," The Alan Lomax Collection, Association for Cultural Equity <http://www.alan-lomax.com/about_StetsonKennedy.html> (April 3, 2006).

9. Hemenway, p. 212.

10. Boyd, p. 280.

11. Hemenway, p. 219.

12. John Guggenheim Memorial Foundation <http://www.gf.org/broch.html#top> April 3, 2006.

13. Kaplan, p. 376.

14. Hurston, p. 169.

15. Zora Neale Hurston, *Tell My Horse* (New York: HarperPerennial, 1996), p. 142.

16. Hurston, *Dust Tracks*, p. 168.

17. Hurston, *Tell My Horse*, p. 158.

Chapter 8. Love Stories

1. Zora Neale Hurston, *Dust Tracks on a Road* (New York: HarperPerennial, 1996), p. 205.

2. Ibid., p. 207.

3. Ibid.

4. Ibid., p. 208.

5. Robert E. Hemenway, *Zora Neale Hurston: A Literary Biography* (Urbana, Ill.: University of Illinois Press, 1980), p. 241.

6. Valerie Boyd, *Wrapped In Rainbows: The Life of Zora Neale Hurston* (New York: Scribner, 2003), p. 306.

7. Hemenway, p. 241.

8. Boyd, p. 307.

9. Ibid.

10. Ibid.

11. Hemenway, p. 242.

12. Carla Kaplan, *Zora Neale Hurston: A Life In Letters* (New York: Doubleday, 2002), p. 403.

13. Zora Neale Hurston, *Tell My Horse* (New York: HarperPerennial, 1990), p. 139.

14. Kaplan, p. 403.

15. Ibid.

16. Boyd, pp. 321–322.

17. Lucy Anne Hurston, *Speak, So You Can Speak Again: The Life of Zora Neale Hurston* (New York: Doubleday, 2004), p. 24.

18. Boyd, p. 327.

19. Lucy Hurston, p. 25.

20. Boyd., pp. 344–345.

21. Ibid., p. 343.

22. Hemenway, p. 278.

23. Ibid., p. 289.

24. Ibid., p. 288.

25. Kaplan, p. 473.

26. Douglas Gilbert, "When Negro Succeeds, South Is Proud, Zora Hurston Says," *The New York World-Telegram*, February 1, 1943.

27. "Zora Hurston Denies Saying Race Better Off in South," *Atlanta Daily World*, March 3, 1943.

28. Roy Wilkins, "The Watch Tower," *Amsterdam News*, February 27, 1943.

29. Hemenway, p. 295.

30. Ibid., p. 298.

Chapter 9. Last Word

1. Carla Kaplan, *Zora Neale Hurston: A Life in Letters* (New York: Doubleday, 2002), p. 501.

2. Ibid., p. 555.

3. Ibid., p. 549.

4. Valerie Boyd, *Wrapped in Rainbows: The Life of Zora Neale Hurston* (New York: Scribner, 2003), p. 386.

5. Kaplan, p. 570.

6. Boyd, p. 395.

7. Worth Tuttle Hedden, "Turpentine and Moonshine," *New York Herald Tribune Weekly Book Review*, October 10, 1948.

8. Boyd, p. 404.

9. Kaplan, p. 647.

10. Ibid., p. 662.

11. Ibid., p. 670.

12. Ibid., p. 552.

13. Boyd., pp. 423–424.

14. Alice Walker, *In Search of Our Mothers' Gardens* (Orlando, Fla.: Harcourt, 1983), p. 107.

15. Kaplan, p. 738.

16. Ibid., p. 746.

17. Ibid., p. 759.

18. Walker, *In Search of Our Mothers' Gardens*, p. 12.

Chapter 10. Loyal to the Language

1. Zora Neale Hurston, *Dust Tracks on a Road* (New York: HarperPerennial, 1996), pp. 175–176.

Further Reading

Brown, Lois. *The Encyclopedia of the Harlem Literary Renaissance*. New York: Facts on File, 2006.

Bryant, Phillip S. *Zora Neale Hurston*. Raintree, 2003.

Campbell, Josie P. *Student Companion to Zora Neale Hurston*. Westport, Conn.: Greenwood Press, 2001.

Cannarella, Deborah. *Zora Neale Hurston: African American Writer*. Chanhazzen, Minn.: Child's World, 2003.

Halpern, Monica. *Moving North: African Americans and the Great Migration, 1915–1930*. Washington, D.C.: National Geographic, 2006.

Hill, Laban Carrick. *Harlem Stomp! A Cultural History of the Harlem Renaissance*. New York: Little Brown, 2003.

Hudson, Wade. *Powerful Words: More Than 200 Years of Extraordinary Writing by African Americans*. New York: Scholastic Nonfiction, 2004.

Hurston, Zora Neale. *Dust Tracks on the Road*. New York: HarperPerennial, 1996.

———. *Folklore, Memoirs, and Other Writings*. New York: Library of America, 1995.

———. *Mules and Men*. New York: HarperPerennial, 1990.

———. *Their Eyes Were Watching God*. New York: HarperCollins, 2000.

Kaplan, Carla, ed. *Zora Neale Hurston: A Life in Letters*. New York: Doubleday, 2002.

Rampersand, Arnold, and David Roessel, eds. *Langston Hughes*. New York: Sterling Publishing, 2006.

Rau, Dana Meachen. *The Harlem Renaissance*. Minneapolis: Compass Point Books, 2006.

Wilkinson, Brenda. *African American Women Writers*. New York: Wiley, 2000.

Internet Addresses

The Zora Neale Hurston Festival of the Arts and Humanities
<http://www.zoranealehurston.cc/>

The Zora Neale Hurston's Plays at the Library of Congress
<http://memory.loc.gov>
Click on "Performing Arts, Music." Scroll down and select "Hurston, Zora Neale~Plays~1925–1944."

Zora Neale Hurston, the WPA in Florida, and the Cross City Turpentine Camp
<http://www.floridamemory.com/onlineclassroom/ zora-hurston>
Click on "Online Classroom" at the left. Select "Go to Exhibits with Lesson Plans." Scroll down and click on "Zora Neale Hurston, the WPA in Florida, and the Cross City Turpentine Camp."

Index

Page numbers for photographs are in **boldface** type.

INDEX